Pedaling ~ Colors in Sound

Lessons and Repertoire for Elementary Piano Students

Katherine Faricy
Music by James P. Callahan

Acknowledgements

ithout the generous contributions of the talents of the following, this book would not have come into being:

Beatriz Aguerrevere — Graphic Design, Web Design
Jon Michael Iverson — Digital Engraver
Kara Ellefson — Editor
Julienne Rasmussen — Artwork and Cover
Katherine Condon — Artwork
Oscar Jockel — Web Design

Also, grateful thanks go to the many teachers who tried out the book with their students and evaluated its contents.

This book is covered by copyright law. Please follow the intention of this law and do not photocopy. Reproduction of any part of this book without the permission of the publisher can lead to prosecution.

6th printing
Copyright©2009 by MaryMark Music

ISBN 9780615288055

TABLE OF CONTENTS

Foreword to Teachers 4

Lesson 1 - How the Piano Works 6
    Piano Mechanism 6
    The Pedals 7

Lesson 2 - Using the Damper Pedal 8
    How the Damper Pedal Works 8
    How to Sit When Using the Damper Pedal 9
    Depressing and Releasing the Damper Pedal 9
    How Pedaling is Shown in Music 9

Lesson 3 - Long Pedals 10
    Dory Ann's Song 11
    Twinkling Stars 12
    The Dungeon 13
    Three O'Clock Bells 14
    The Cuckoo in a Dark Forest 15

Lesson 4 - Direct Pedal 16
    March 17
    Drums and Trumpets 18
    Turkish Dance 19
    Arm and Hammer 20
    My Toy Auto 21
    Sally's Slow Waltz (Duet) 22

Lesson 5 - Syncopated Pedal 25
    Sunny Day 27
    Paddle and Dive 29
    Starting to Dream 30
    Graceful Greek Dancers (Duet) 32
    Tweedledum and Tweedledee 34

Lesson 6 - Slow Pedal Release 35
    Ghost Tones and Three Knocks 36

Lesson 7 - Using the Soft Pedal 37
    Echo 38
    Nocturne With a Bird 39
    Impressions 40

Foreword to Teachers

Systematic Approach
The purpose of this book is to give teachers and students an organized, systematic, and progressive procedure for developing artistic pedaling from the very beginning of piano study.

Develop Tonal Awareness and Imagination
An additional objective of this book is to encourage students to listen carefully and really take notice of the sounds they are producing.

Procedure
To use this book most effectively, it is recommended that all students start at the beginning and then proceed at their own rate through the exercises and repertoire.

WHEN TO START PEDALING?
This book helps teachers introduce pedaling **right from the start of a student's piano study:**

- Introduces **long pedals** first as they do not require any complicated coordination of hands and feet.
- Uses graphic pedal notation.
- Provides important **preparatory exercises** for the students to explore pedal techniques before they incorporate the techniques in repertoire.
- Many of the early studies and pieces **can be taught by rote** so that the use of the pedal can begin before a student can read.

TEACHING SUGGESTIONS FOR LESSONS

Lesson 1 – How the Piano Works
It will be helpful to explain and demonstrate the piano mechanism and pedal actions while the student looks inside the piano. Similarities and differences between grand and upright pianos should also be discussed.

Lesson 2 – Using the Damper Pedal
How to Sit When Using the Pedal
  Students tall enough to easily reach the pedals should sit as described in the book on page 9.

  Small Students
  For students who cannot reach the pedals, the following solutions are offered:

- Initially, the **Teacher** may pedal for the student in order to introduce the pedaled sonorities.
- The small student can use the damper pedal while they are essentially **standing up and leaning against the bench.** They can develop normal posture (with a box under their feet for support) while practicing technique and pieces that aren't pedaled.
- Ideally, teacher and students will purchase and use a **pedal extender box.**

How the Damper Pedal Works
- When the student speaks or sings into the piano with the damper pedal depressed, they can hear the piano sounds **like an echo chamber.** (If doing this demonstration on an **upright piano**, the top can be opened but the student is likely to need a little step ladder or chair to be tall enough to shout down into the strings.)
- Invite students to **improvise with the damper pedal down** by suggesting certain kinds of sounds for them to make, utilizing the **different registers, different dynamic levels and moods.** (Again, if they are too small to reach the pedals, the teacher can depress the pedal down for them.)
- To help students connect their imaginations with tonal colors, **suggest different things for them to imitate in sound,** such as thunder, raindrops, birds, butterflies, monsters, etc.

Lesson 3 – Long Pedals

Use: To blend sonorities together, which is a common effect in music in the Impressionist style.

Technique:
- Long pedal technique is the simplest one of all.
- This lesson introduces how to **depress and release the pedal properly,** and also how to **blend sounds together** in a long pedal.
- Students must be reminded to always **listen intently** to sonority and dynamics.

Lesson 4 – Simultaneous (Direct) Pedal

Use: to **enhance** the dynamic and tonal quality of a **single note or chord** or a passagework unit such as an **arpeggio, scale or trill.**

Technique:
- Students will become comfortable with using **both their hands and feet** in a simple, precise and rhythmic way as they work together in the **same direction at the same time.**
- Before using this pedal technique in pieces, The *Pedal Studies* must be practiced until the student can **coordinate** the hand and foot with **comfort, accuracy and steadiness.**
- Be sure that the **application** and **release** of the pedal occur **exactly** where indicated in the studies and in the pieces.

Lesson 5 – Syncopated Pedal

Uses: This technique is used in **legato** passages.

- It can be used to enhance the **quality of sound,** warming the tone much in the same way *vibrato* does in the violin and other instruments.
- It can be used in accompanied melodies and for connecting legato chords.
- The pedal should **not be used** to substitute for a good finger legato.

Technique:
- Students need to learn to **pedal precisely in time,** with the foot acting somewhat like a human metronome.
- It is important for the student to **complete all of the** *Pedal Studies* before trying to apply this more demanding technique in a piece.
- When the students feel **comfortable** and are able to do the exercises **easily,** they can proceed to the pieces in this book and should begin to add pedal to other pieces as well.

Lesson 6 – Slow Pedal Release

Use: Releases of a note or chord with the pedal create a **more beautiful ending** to a sound than the release of notes or chords with the fingers. With a pedal release, the dampers can be returned to the strings more gently and make a more tapered ending to the sound.

Technique:
- After mastering the *Pedal Studies* and the pieces in this lesson, the student should apply this technique to the endings of pieces like those found on pages 10, 11, 13, 14, 24.

Lesson 7 – Using the Soft Pedal

Use: to change the color, or quality of the sound, as well as to aid in soft dynamics.

(In addition to the pieces in this lesson, the student should apply this pedaling technique to other pieces in this book and other repertoire where the use of this pedal will enhance the color and effect.)

Technique:
- Remind students to depress the soft pedal before the notes or section where it is to be used.

For more information on pedaling technique, see:

Faricy, Katherine. *Artistic Pedal Technique: Lessons for Intermediate and Advanced Pianists.* Frederick Harris Music, Mississauga, Ontario, Canada.

Lesson 1 - How the Piano Works

The piano is a wonderful instrument to learn to play because it can do so many things - it can "sing" or sound like an orchestra; it can sound scary like a lion's roar or soft like the wind; it can imitate elephants and birds or anything else you can imagine!

Piano Mechanism

There are two basic types of acoustic pianos:

Upright Piano

Grand Piano

Look inside the piano and you will see how it works:

Strings
For each piano key, there are one to three strings. When strings vibrate they make a musical pitch or sound.

Hammers
When we depress a piano key, a little felt-covered hammer inside the piano pops up and strikes the string causing it to vibrate.

Dampers
A set of dampers sits on top of the strings to keep them from vibrating. When a key is depressed the damper lifts at the same time the hammer strikes the string. The damper stays up until you let go of the key. When it drops back down on the string it stops the vibration and silences the sound.

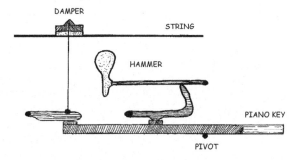
Grand Piano Mechanism

(An upright piano is built differently than a grand piano as you can see, but the strings, hammers and dampers work pretty much the same.)

The Pedals

Most pianos have three pedals. Each pedal affects the sound in a different way.

The *Damper* Pedal (Right Pedal)
When the damper pedal is depressed, it lifts all of the dampers on the keyboard even though no keys are played.

The *Una Corda* Pedal (Left Pedal)
This pedal is sometimes called the soft pedal. When it is depressed, it changes the color of the sound, and also causes the sound to be softer.

The *Sostenuto* Pedal (Middle Pedal)
This pedal is sometimes called the "sustain pedal." When you hold notes down and then depress this pedal, it keeps the dampers up for just these notes, allowing them to continue to sound after you release the keys.

As long as you keep this pedal down, you can then play other notes which will stop sounding when you lift your fingers. To try this effect, play the following:

Sostenuto: ↓

Be sure to put the *sostenuto* pedal down after you play the low G and while you are still holding it down with your finger. The low G will continue to sound until you lift the sostenuto pedal.

The *sostenuto* pedal is not used very often. This book does not contain any studies using this pedal, other than the one above. On some upright pianos, the middle pedal is not a *sostenuto* pedal at all, but is a "**practice pedal**." The "practice pedal" has **no musical purpose** - it just mutes the sound so you don't disturb anyone while practicing.

Pedaling - Colors in Sound   Lesson 1

Lesson 2 - Using the Damper Pedal

The **damper pedal** is the most used of the three pedals. This book will introduce you to some of its many possibilities, and will help you develop the control you need to use this pedal effectively.

How the Damper Pedal Works

1. Ask your teacher to depress the pedal while you look inside the piano to see how this works.
   - You will see that when the pedal is depressed, the dampers raise, which will allow the strings vibrate.
   - When the pedal is released, the dampers return to the strings.

2. With the lid of the piano raised, place your head inside the piano and **slowly shout "Hello"** into the strings!

3. Ask your teacher to depress the damper pedal and then shout "Hello" into the strings again. **Listen** to the sound of your voice in the piano after you quit shouting. An '**echo**' occurs because when the pedal is down, it holds the dampers off of the strings so that your voice can make all of the strings vibrate.

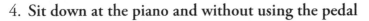

4. **Sit down at the piano and without using the pedal**
   - **Play** a key in the middle of the keyboard with a full sound, and hold it for about **4 counts.**
   - **Listen** carefully to the sound and what happens to it when you **release** the key and the dampers return to the strings.

5. **Depress the damper pedal**
   - **Play** the same note, holding it for about two counts.
   - **Keep** the pedal down when you **release** the key.
   - **Listen** to how the note you played continues to sound for a long time when the pedal remains depressed.

6. **Release the pedal all of the way.** The dampers will then rest on the strings, **stopping the sound.**

7. **Play the note again without the damper pedal**, and listen to the difference.

How to Sit When Using the Damper Pedal

1. Sit on the **front** of the bench, with your body balanced equally between your "sitting" bones and your feet. Be sure you are sitting tall.

2. Place your right foot on the pedal, touching the part of the pedal closest to you with the ball of your foot.

3. Your heel should be firmly on the floor and aligned directly behind the pedal.

Depressing and Releasing the Damper Pedal

1. Keep your foot in the position described above and slowly **depress** the pedal, keeping your **heel** on the **floor** at all times.

2. **Release** the pedal by lifting the ball of your foot up slowly, letting the pedal return to its resting position. Be careful **not to let the pedal pop up uncontrolled,** or you will hear a big thunk!

3. Make sure the ball of your foot **stays in contact** with the pedal at all times. Imagine the bottom of your shoe is attached to the pedal with glue!

How Pedaling is Shown in Music

In most music books, there are special marks that indicate where the pedal is to be depressed and released. The marks look like the illustrations below:

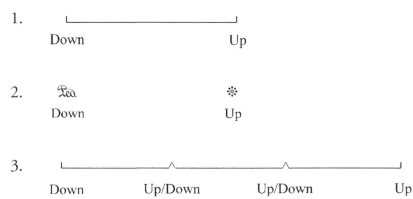

In this book, all of the above ways of indicating pedal will be used. In addition, the downs and ups of the pedal will be shown like this:

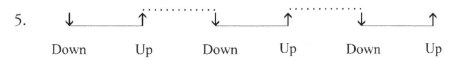

Lesson 3 - Long Pedals

When we hold the damper pedal down while we play, we can make beautiful colors and interesting sounds that can create all kinds of pictures and feelings in our imaginations.

Pedal Study 1

Depress the pedal, **then play one note** and **listening carefully** to the sound as it gradually fades away (decays).

Pedal Study 2 'Nest of Boxes'

Boxes of different sizes that fit one inside of the other are called a 'nest of boxes', like this:

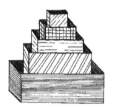

We play musical 'nest of boxes' **when each new note or chord is softer** (like a smaller box) than the sound left by the previous chord.

Pedal Study 3

Note to teacher:
The first note in the left hand is the "big box." Make sure it is played loud enough to fit all of the other sounds inside. Have student keep listening to the "big box" throughout.

Note to teacher:

This piece is in the Dorian mode.
- *Think of the nest of boxes - pay close attention to the dynamics.*
- *Listen to the long notes as they fade away. (The long notes in ms. 2,4,6,8, may be held longer than written.)*

Dory Ann's Song

James P. Callahan

PEDALING - COLORS IN SOUND

Lesson 3

Note to teacher:

- *Remind the student to think of the "Nest of Boxes."*
- *Depress pedal before playing.*
- *Play the bass notes (the big boxes) with a full sound and keep listening to them throughout the piece.*
- *Play the 'twinkles' in the right hand with very short staccatos. Observe the dynamics.*
- *This piece can be played as written and then immediately repeated one octave higher, without changing the pedal.*

Twinkling Stars

Hand position

James P. Callahan

(sempre Ped.)

Pedaling - Colors in Sound

Lesson 3

Helpful hints:

- Before you start to play, think of how it would feel to be in a deep dark dungeon with creepy crawly things!
- The piano can make scary sounds!

The Dungeon

Hand position

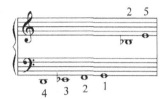

James P. Callahan

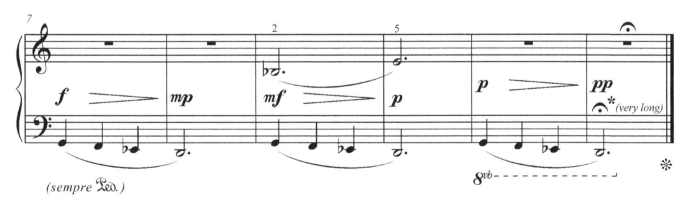

(sempre Ped.)

* *Hold fermata for a very long time (at least the equivalent of eight measures).*

PEDALING - COLORS IN SOUND   Lesson 3

Depress the pedal before beginning to play; release the pedal after the sound dies away.

Three O'Clock Bells

Hand position

James P. Callahan

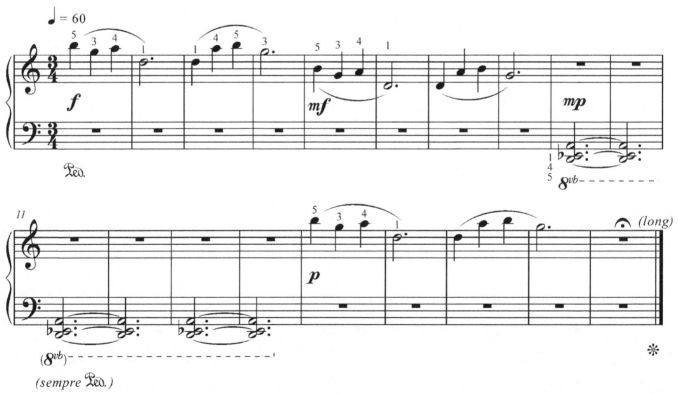

Pedaling - Colors in Sound

Lesson 3

The Cuckoo in a Dark Forest

Hand position

James P. Callahan

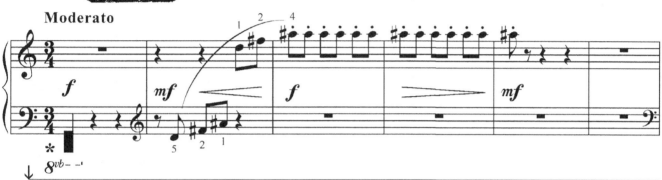

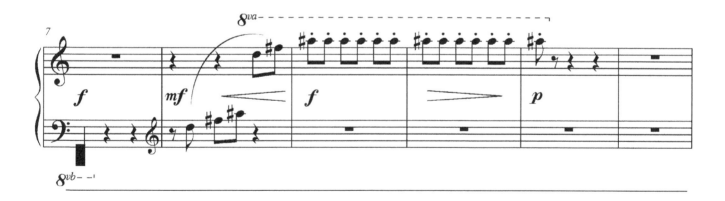

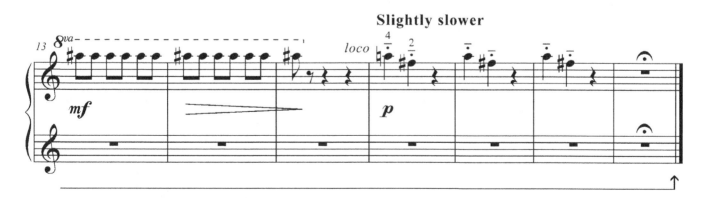

* *Measures 1 & 7: Cluster chords (to be played with the palm of hand).*

PEDALING - COLORS IN SOUND

Lesson 3

Lesson 4 - Direct Pedal

Note to teacher:
The direct pedal technique is where the hand and foot work together in the same direction. When the hand plays the keys, the right foot goes down. When the hand releases the keys, the foot returns to the "up" position. Have the students practice the following studies until they can do them easily.

Pedal Study 1 – without pedal

- Sit on the edge of the piano bench, with both feet flat on the floor and one hand on each thigh.
- Bring your right hand off of your leg and lift the ball of your right foot off the floor exactly at the same time. Keep your heel on the floor.
- Put your hand and foot back down exactly together.
- Repeat these motions, saying Up and Down. Keep a steady beat.

- Repeat the exercise using the left hand and right foot.
- Repeat using both hands and right foot.

Pedal Study 2 – with pedal

- Place your right foot on the damper pedal with your right hand on your thigh as you did in Pedal Study 1.
- Do the same movements as above, but depress and release the pedal with your foot. (Be sure to keep your right heel on the floor.)
- Your hand should go up and down at exactly the same time as the pedal does. Continue to say Up and Down with the movements.
- Repeat this using the left hand.
- Repeat using both hands.

Pedal Study 3

Note to teacher:
- *Have student count "1-2-3" instead of saying "Up" and "Down." Have them count aloud.*
- *The pedal and the key both go down on count 1 and up on count 3 as indicated in the pedal notation.*
- *Be sure the student's right heel stays on the floor when the pedal is depressed, and that the ball of the right foot remains on the pedal when it is released.*

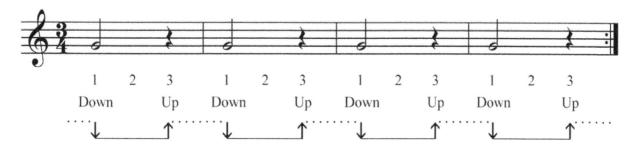

March

Hand position

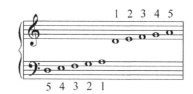

James P. Callahan

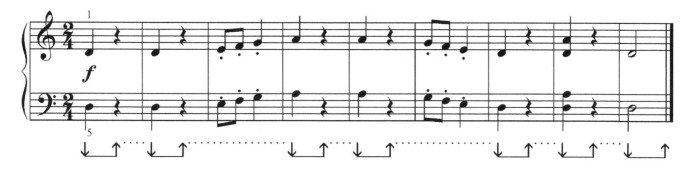

PEDALING - COLORS IN SOUND   Lesson 4

Turkish Dance

James P. Callahan

PEDALING - COLORS IN SOUND

Lesson 4

Arm and Hammer

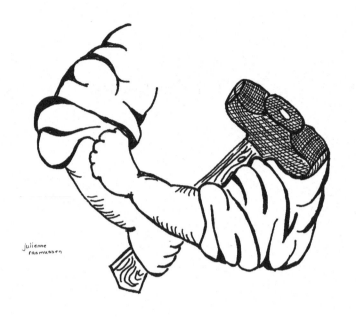

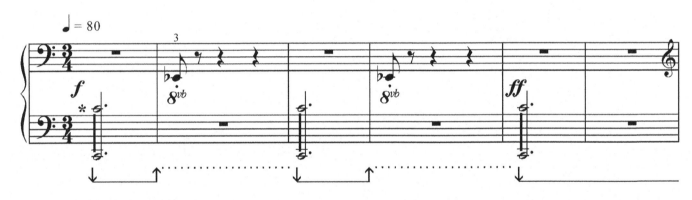

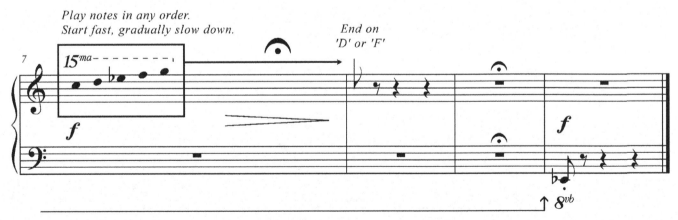

* Play with left forearm on white keys
** Keep repeating the notes in the box in any order until the end of the arrow.

PEDALING - COLORS IN SOUND

Lesson 4

Note to teacher:

Student chooses the order of the phrases. Phrase 2 will always be in the middle. So, ① ② ③ or ③ ② ①.
Repeat each phrase as desired.

My Toy Auto

James P. Callahan

PEDALING - COLORS IN SOUND

Lesson 4

Sally's Slow Waltz (Duet)

James P. Callahan

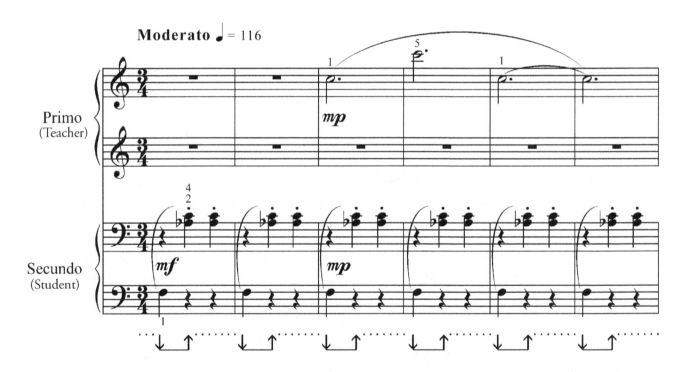

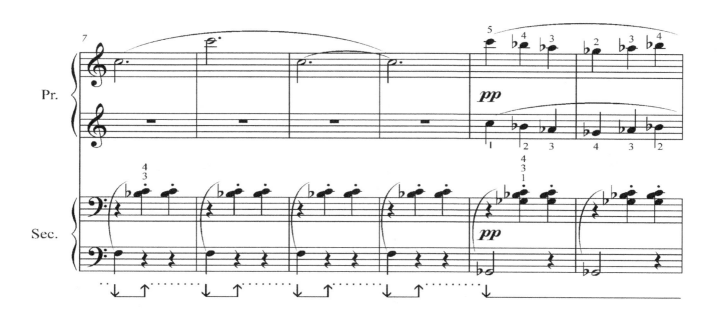
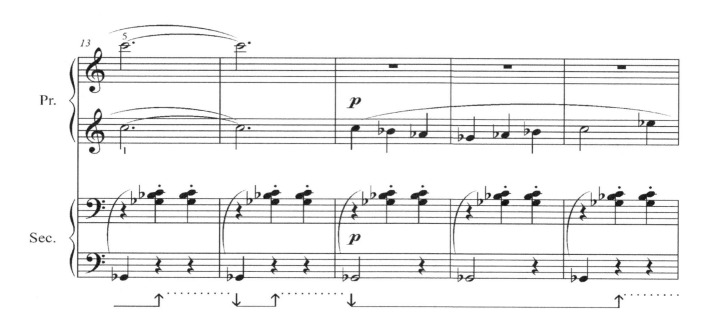

Pedaling - Colors in Sound

Lesson 4

24

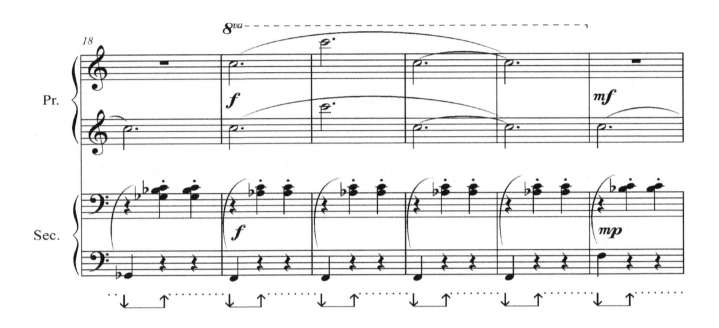

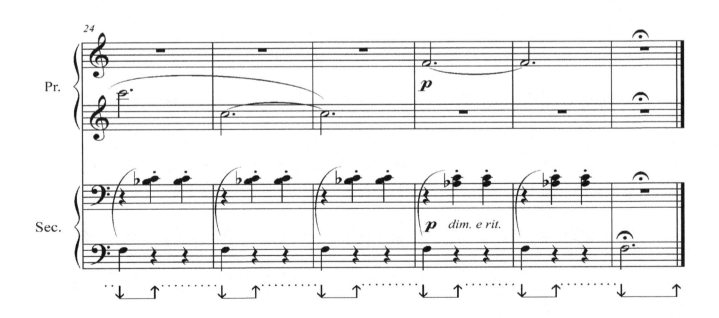

Lesson 5 - Syncopated Pedal

Note to teacher:
The syncopated pedal technique is where the hand and the sole of the foot work in opposite directions. When the hand goes down, the sole of the foot goes up; when the hand goes up, the sole of the foot goes down – exactly at the same time.

Syncopated pedaling works a little like those trash cans where the lid goes up when the foot pushes down on a pedal:

Pedal Study 1

1. Sit on the edge of the piano bench with both feet on the floor and your right hand on your right thigh.

2. Raise the big toe of your right foot off the floor, keeping your right heel down. Now **pretend you are using the trash can:**

   - Push the pedal down with your toe. Bring your right hand (the 'lid' of the can) up off your leg at the same time.

   - Then put your right hand back down and bring your toe (the 'pedal') up at the same time.

3. Repeat the movements keeping time with a metronome set at ♩ = 60

4. Repeat using the left hand with right foot.

Pedal Study 2 *(For foot movements only)*

- Sit at the piano with your foot resting on the damper pedal. **Depress and release the pedal keeping time with your foot movements.** Be as steady as a metronome.
- **Say the words** "up" and "down" (and "hold") as your foot moves. Be sure to keep the foot in contact with the pedal at all times.

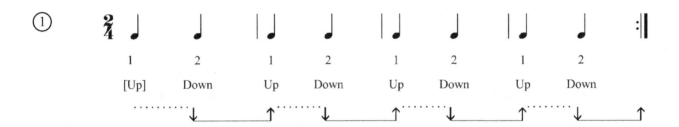

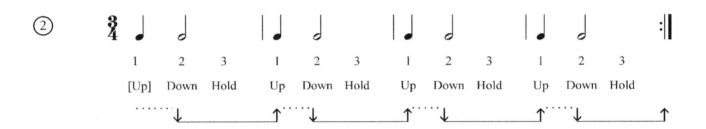

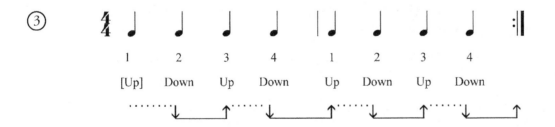

- **Repeat** – This time say the **beat numbers out loud**. Notice that the pedal is **always depressed** on the count of **2**, and always released on the count of **1**.

Pedal Study 3

Note to teacher:
*In the following study, notes played on the keyboard are combined with the use of the pedal. Be sure the student **counts out loud and keeps strict time with both hand and foot**. Notice that in this example and others, **the hand goes down as the foot goes up, but the hand does not come up when the foot goes down.***

Sunny Day

James P. Callahan

PEDALING - COLORS IN SOUND — Lesson 5

Pedal Study 4

In this study you need to count eighth notes even if you aren't playing them with your fingers. Remember there are two eighths in every quarter note:

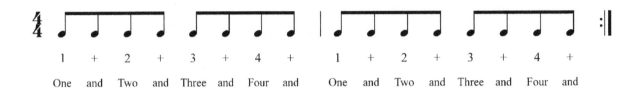

1. Count the following:

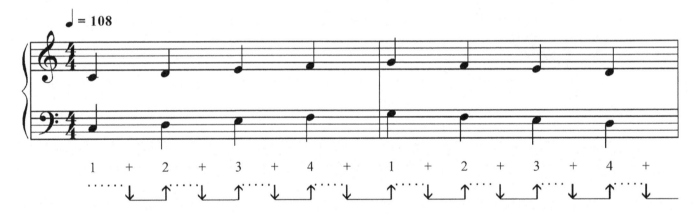

2. Play the following:

   - When you say the *count number*, the **finger** goes **down** and at the exact same time, the **pedal** goes **up**.
   - When you say "*and*", the **pedal** goes **down**.

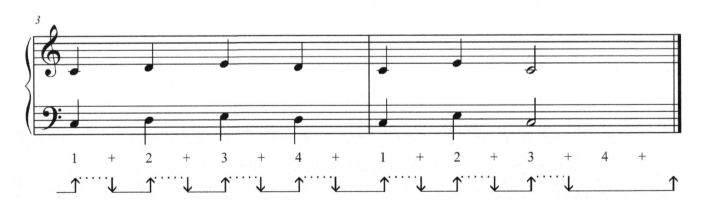

Starting to Dream

James P. Callahan

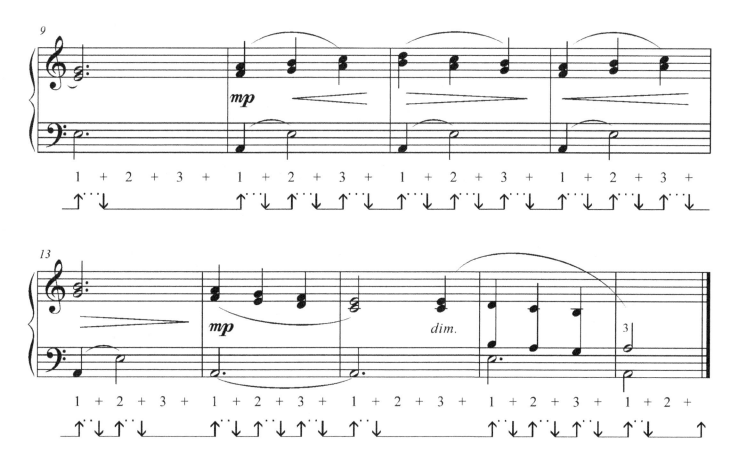

PEDALING - COLORS IN SOUND

Lesson 5

Graceful Greek Dancers (Duet)

James P. Callahan

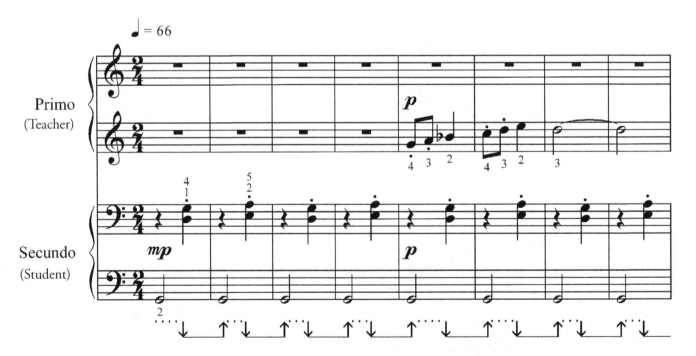

PEDALING - COLORS IN SOUND

Lesson 5

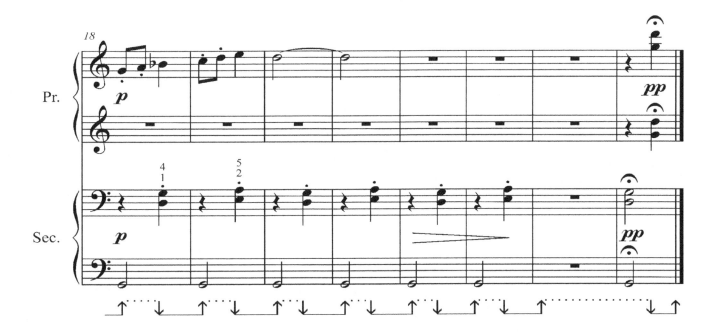

Pedaling - Colors in Sound

Lesson 5

Note to teacher:
In measures 6-13, be sure the student connects the chords cleanly with the pedal when the hands change positions.

PEDALING - COLORS IN SOUND

Lesson 5

Lesson 6 - Slow Pedal Release

Sometimes we want the sound to slowly die away—as in a slow and soft ending of a piece. We can accomplish this with a beautiful effect by bringing the pedal up very slowly after releasing the notes with the hand.

Pedal Study 1

- Play the following study and listen carefully as the sounds slowly get softer as you slowly release the pedal in each measure. The sound is finished with the release of the pedal, not when the chord is released by the hand on the 3rd beat.

- Take as much time as you want at the end of each measure.

- Be careful to move the pedal **very slowly as it nears the top,** because this is when the dampers are getting close to the strings and begin to stop the vibrations and sound.

- Notice that the gradual release of the pedal is indicated by the upward arrow.

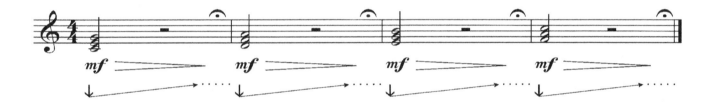

Pedal Study 2

A Very Important Trick!
- When you release the chord in the second measure, do it secretly, so no one sees you do it. Audiences sometimes 'listen' with their eyes! If you don't move a muscle, they will concentrate on the disappearing sound and experience the mood it creates.

- After you have released the keys, start lifting the pedal very slowly.

- Don't move your hand, arms, head or body until long after the sound is gone.

- Remove your hands from the piano very slowly, and gently put them in your lap. This way, you won't ruin the mood of the soft ending.

Note to teacher:

* *In addition to the pieces that follows, almost any pieces that end quietly and slowly can use this slow pedal release. Go back to the pieces on pages 10, 11, 13, 14, 24, and play the endings with a slow pedal release.*
* *The "ghost tones" in this piece are a result of sympathetic vibrations.*

Ghost Tones and Three Knocks

James P. Callahan

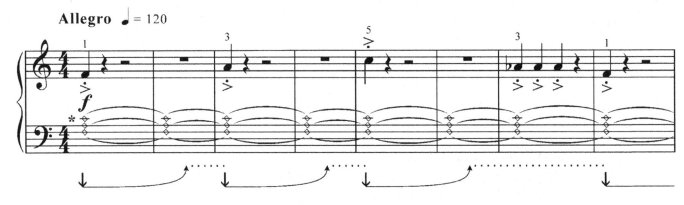

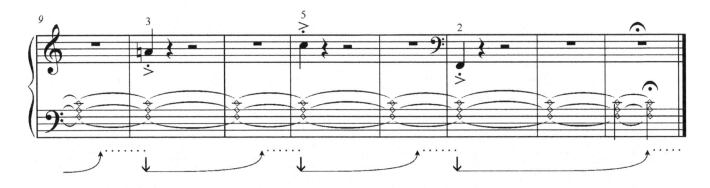

* Before you begin playing the right hand notes, depress the keys
  in the left hand silently and hold down throughout the piece.

PEDALING - COLORS IN SOUND

Lesson 5

Lesson 7 - Using the Soft Pedal

When we depress this pedal, which is also known as the *una corda* pedal, the hammers are moved in such a way that they strike the strings differently. On a grand piano, the hammers are moved sideways so that they only strike two of the three strings, which changes the color of the sound and also causes it to be softer.

To hear this effect, do the following:

1. Play this softly:

2. Now depress the soft pedal, and play again. Listen carefully to the sound:

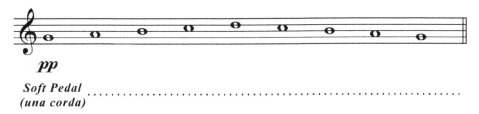

Note to teacher:
- *The main purpose of this pedal is to change the color of the sound, not just to soften the sound. You can play loudly and use this pedal to change the color too!*
- *This pedal must be depressed right **before** playing the section where the color change is wanted.*
- *This pedal is called the "una corda" pedal, which means "one string" in Italian. On a grand piano the damper mechanism shifts so the dampers strike fewer strings. On the early pianos, it shifted so it actually struck only one string – thus the name, "una corda." [On an upright piano, the hammers do not shift, but rather are moved closer to the strings when the pedal is depressed, which results in a color change and softer sound.]*
- *When we release the "una corda pedal", it goes back to striking three strings, which is "tre corde" in Italian.*
- *When composers wants the soft pedal depressed, they indicate this by writing "U.C." below the staff; "T.C." indicates the point at which the pedal is to be released.*

Music Pieces

In these next pieces, you will use:

1. The soft pedal
2. The damper pedal
3. A slow pedal release at the end of each piece.

Remember To Paint Pictures In Your Sounds!

Echo

James P. Callahan

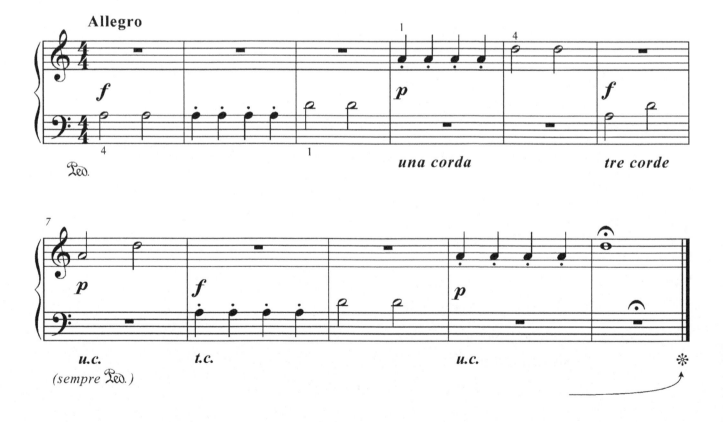

PEDALING - COLORS IN SOUND

Lesson 5

Nocturne With a Bird

Hand position

James P. Callahan

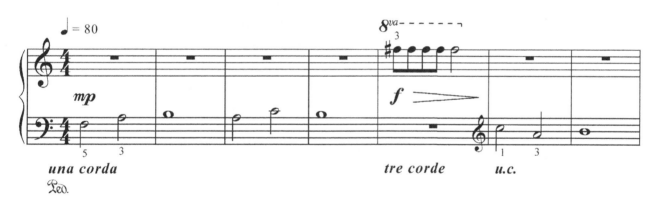

una corda   *tre corde*   *u.c.*

(*sempre Ped.*)   *t.c.*   *u.c.*

PEDALING - COLORS IN SOUND   Lesson 7

Be careful to follow dynamics indicated.

Impressions

James P. Callahan

The Author

KATHERINE FARICY

Katherine Faricy graduated from the Oberlin College Conservatory of Music with a bachelor's degree in music education and received her master of fine arts degree in piano performance from the University of Minnesota. She also studied privately for four years with the renowned concert pianist, Madame Lili Kraus. It was during studies with Kraus and Dr. Duncan McNab at the U of M that she became very aware of the importance of pedaling in artistic performance and how few people are taught a methodical approach to learning its technique. Her unique book, *Artistic Pedal Technique-Lessons for Intermediate and Advanced Pianists* published by Frederick Harris Music Co., has become an international success.

While on the piano faculty for many years at the University of St. Thomas in St Paul, MN, Faricy taught undergraduate and graduate piano and courses in performance practices and piano pedagogy. She currently is Artist-in-Residence at Mount Calvary Academy of Music in Excelsior, MN, where she teaches piano and gives seminars for piano teachers. A frequent recitalist and soloist with orchestras, she also performed with Dr. James Callahan as an acclaimed duo-piano team for 30 years. Katherine Faricy is in frequent demand as an adjudicator and clinician, giving workshops and lecture/demonstrations to many teachers' groups throughout the country including MTNA national conventions.

The Composer

JAMES P. CALLAHAN

Dr. James Callahan earned a BA from St. John's University (MN) followed by an MFA in piano and a Ph.D. in music theory and composition from the University of Minnesota. In addition he studied at the Salzburg Mozarteum and the Vienna Academy of Music. After 38 years of teaching piano, organ, music theory, composition, and piano literature at the University of St. Thomas, St. Paul, MN, he retired and was named Professor Emeritus of Music.

Dr. Callahan has composed over one hundred twenty-five works for piano, organ, orchestra, band, opera, and chamber ensembles. His works have been performed both by the Minnesota Orchestra and The Saint Paul Chamber Orchestra, and many have been published by McLaughlin-Reilly, GIA, Paraclete Press, Abingdon Press, and Beautiful Star Publishing. He has performed numerous solo piano and ensemble recitals and made many concerto appearances, including all five piano concertos by Beethoven. He and Katherine Faricy performed as a duo piano team. As an organist, Callahan has performed numerous recitals in the upper Midwest, New York and Austria. His performances and compositions have been broadcast on Minnesota Public Radio and on the nationally-broadcast radio program "Pipedreams."

ENDORSEMENTS

"At last piano teachers have a resource to explain sophisticated pedal techniques from the early stages of piano study! Katherine Faricy's *Pedaling–Colors in Sound* contains thorough explanations, creative exercises and wonderfully imaginative compositions by James Callahan that students will enjoy learning. This book will be a welcome addition to our 'Books all Piano Teachers Should Own' list we provide our piano pedagogy students at Westminster Choir College of Rider University."

                INGRID CLARFIELD, Professor of Piano and Piano Pedagogy at Westminster Choir College of Rider University, performer, clinician, and author.

"For teachers looking for an effective tool to help students develop the awareness, imagination, skills, and vocabulary of artistic pedaling from the earliest lessons, *Pedaling–Colors in Sound* is a flexible and practical—and delightful!— resource. Easy to use with any course of study, this compact volume gives structure and focus to learning to pedal with precision, confidence, and artistry. A welcome pre-quel to Faricy's *Artistic Pedal Technique: Lessons For Intermediate and Advanced Pianists*."

                ANDREW HISEY, pianist, teacher, clinician, and pedagogy consultant; editor and senior examiner for the Royal Conservatory of Music.

"*Pedaling–Colors in Sound*, by pianist-pedagogue Katherine Faricy and composer James Callahan provides piano teachers with a rich treasure trove of concise information, imaginative exercises and delightful short pieces. These introduce students to artistic pedaling from the very beginning of their piano study. The book is a welcome contribution that teachers will find indispensable!"

                PHYLLIS LEHRER, Professor of Piano and Piano Pedagogy at Westminster Choir College of Rider University, performer, clinician, and author.

"I can think of a thousand uses for *Pedaling–Colors in Sound* in my own studio! It will become the new standard for teaching artistic pedaling."

                SCOTT MCBRIDE SMITH, Cordelia Brown Murphy Professor of Piano Pedagogy School of Music, University of Kansas.

"Here is a book that will be a life-saver for teachers and students dealing with introducing the pianist's 'third hand.' The simple, short exercises that introduce the different types of pedaling are invaluable. What a gift to any teacher and student to have these written out in a fun and accessible manner. I cannot overemphasize the necessity of correct and sequential pedal introduction from the earliest stage. As a composer, I incorporate different pedaling opportunities in my pieces for students. Katherine Faricy's book will definitely be a part of my studio!"

                CHEE-HWA TAN, composer of student pieces, performer, and teacher.

GLOSSARY

𝄢. sempre	Literal translation: "pedal always". Hold the damper pedal throughout the entire piece, or until change or *
(sempre 𝄢.)	A courtesy reminder placed at the beginning of the second line: continue to hold damper pedal throughout.

1. [cluster chord notation] 2. [cluster chord notation]	Cluster chords: large groups of pitches that are played simultaneously. This notation includes both white and black notes.
	
	In these pieces, you are to play the cluster chords one of two ways:
	    1. With the palm of the LH, or
	    2. With forearm of the left arm.

8va- - - - - ⌐	*All' ottava* – "at the octave". Play the notes below the bracket an octave higher than written.
8vb- - - - - ⌐	*Ottava bassa* – "at the octave below". Play the notes above the bracket an octave lower than written.
15ma- - - - - ⌐	*Quindicesima* – "at the fifteenth". Play the notes below the bracket two octaves higher than written.
loco	"at place" – The notes are to be played at pitch. This is a courtesy to remind the performer that the *8va*, *8vb* or *15ma* no longer applies.
① ② ③ ③ ② ①	Module notation: the performer chooses the order in which the sections of the piece are to be played. In this case, the performer may choose 1, 2, 3 or 3, 2, 1.
[silently depressed keys notation]	Silently depress the keys.
[three pedal release notations]	Gradual pedal releases. Is notated three different ways.
una corda - u.c.	*una corda* – depress the left pedal (soft pedal). Abbreviated <u>u.c.</u>
tre corde – t.c.	*tre corde* – release the left pedal (soft pedal). Abbreviated <u>t.c.</u>
[boxed notes with fermata and arrow]	

Made in the USA
Coppell, TX
20 February 2020

16000329R00026